WINTER'S TAIL

How One Little Dolphin Learned to Swim Again

Told by JULIANA HATKOFF,
ISABELLA HATKOFF, *and* CRAIG HATKOFF

SCHOLASTIC INC.
New York Toronto London Auckland
Sydney Mexico City New Delhi Hong Kong

We dedicate this book to the millions of children around the world who struggle with disabilities of all kinds and to all children who might learn from Winter that through resilience, compassion, and friendship, they can help make the world a better place for everyone.

Authors' Note: We are fortunate to have the actual rescue photographs for this book taken while Winter's ordeal was unfolding. While these photos are not high resolution, the mere fact that they were recorded at all gives us a valuable insight into the drama of this extraordinary event.

Text copyright © 2009 by Turtle Pond Publications LLC.
Endpaper illustration copyright © 2009 by Isabella Hatkoff, used by permission.

Photo credits: Front and back cover photographs © J Carrier. Pages 4, 8, 9 © J Carrier. Pages 10, 14–17 © Clearwater Marine Aquarium. Page 11 © Jim Savage. Pages 12, 13 © Harbor Branch Oceanic Institute. Pages 18–33 © J Carrier. Map on page 34: Courtesy of Jim McMahon.

This book was originally published by Scholastic Press in 2009.

ISBN 978-0-545-34830-0

12 11 10 9 8 7 6 5 4   12 13 14 15/0

Printed in the U.S.A.   08 · First Scholastic paperback printing, August 2011

Book design by Elizabeth B. Parisi · The text was set in Adobe Garamond.

We would like to thank everyone at the Clearwater Marine Aquarium and all those who helped in the rescue and rehabilitation of Winter for their unending dedication and for sharing her story with the world. We would also like to thank Jennifer Rees, J Carrier, Kristen Earhart, Laura Morgan, Rachel Mandel, and our mom, Jane Rosenthal. And of course we would like to thank Winter, who is an inspiration to the world.

For more information about our growing collection of true animal stories, please visit www.turtlepondpublications.com, www.owenandmzee.com, www.knut.net, www.miza.com and www.scholastic.com/miza, www.leothesnowleopard.com, and www.winterstail.com and www.scholastic.com/winterstail.

Dear Friends,

You may be familiar with our growing collection of remarkable true stories from around the world about young animals facing adversity: a baby hippo (Owen) orphaned during the Asian tsunami and adopted and raised by a 130-year-old giant tortoise (Mzee); a baby polar bear (Knut) abandoned at birth by his mother and hand-raised by a caring zookeeper at the Berlin Zoo; and a suddenly motherless baby mountain gorilla (Miza) lost in the jungles of the Democratic Republic of Congo, rescued by her brave father, a fierce silverback (Kabirizi) who brought Miza back home, where she is now being raised by her sister (Tumaini) and half brother (Mivumbi).

We are now pleased to introduce you to another remarkable true story—unlike our other, land-based tales, this one rises from the sea. This is the story of Winter, a young female bottlenose dolphin who injures and then loses her tail after being mangled in a crab trap off the coast of Florida. Dolphins normally propel themselves at great speeds with incredible agility, using an up-and-down motion of their fanlike tails. The injured Winter is rescued and brought to the Clearwater Marine Aquarium, where she at first adjusts and learns to swim without her tail by moving her body with a side-to-side motion. Winter's natural and cleverly improvised solution creates grave concern amongst her caretakers because it is clear to them that she is injuring her spine and internal organs with this effective but inelegant method of propulsion, which would only compound over time as she grew.

The solution to this dire problem came from the miracle of modern technology. A tireless group of dedicated prosthetic engineers devised a prosthetic tail that enables Winter to once again swim like a dolphin. This is a story of ingenuity and perseverance—both human and animal. Winter has already become an inspiration and an icon for millions touched directly and indirectly by all types of challenges. We hope you enjoy Winter's Tail, *the poignant story of one brave little dolphin who learned how to swim again.*

With love and hope,

Craig Hatkoff   Juliana Hatkoff   Isabella Hatkoff

One cold winter morning, just off the east coast of Florida, a baby female dolphin managed to get tangled up in a crab trap. In the effort to free herself, the dolphin caused the ropes securing the crab trap to the buoy to become wrapped around her tail. The more she struggled, the tighter the ropes became, quickly strangling her tail. Luckily, a nearby fisherman caught a glimpse of this unusual situation and came to set the little dolphin free. It was not clear she would survive. And even if she did survive, how would a dolphin manage without a tail? How would she swim? How would she thrive?

Life without her tail would cause many challenges, but with the help and care of a great number of dedicated people, a dolphin named Winter would beat the odds. In return, Winter's story would inspire and warm the hearts of people all over the world.

December 10, 2005, was a chilly Saturday. Jim Savage was the only fisherman braving the bitter wind in Mosquito Lagoon that morning. As Jim steered his boat in the dim light, he noticed a line of crab traps rigged just beneath the water's surface. One trap seemed to be going in a direction opposite from the others. Something was pulling it against the strong wind. Jim idled his boat and steered slowly toward the trap. Even before he could see anything, he heard a harsh, rasping sound over the sound of the waves. When he searched the murky water, Jim found a baby dolphin gasping for breath. She was caught. A rope from the trap was wrapped tightly around both her mouth and tail.

The dolphin was so tangled in the rope that her small body was curled like a horseshoe, her mouth pulled close to her tail. Jim spoke to her, assuring her that he was there to help. He knew he needed to free her head first so she could raise her blowhole out of the water and breathe normally. The dolphin struggled as Jim used his fish-cleaning knife to cut the line that tied her mouth and tail together.

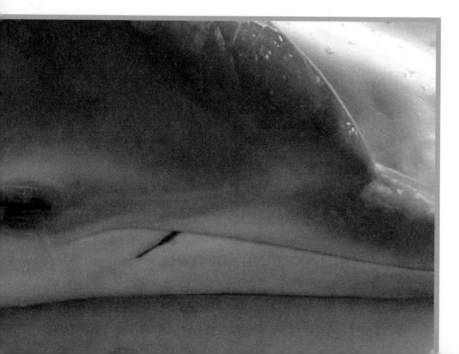

Winter is safe, but is exhausted from her struggle.

Several minutes later, Jim pulled off the last of the rope, and the young dolphin swam away from the boat. She kept her distance from the fisherman, but she did not leave the lagoon. After thirty minutes, Jim understood that she was too exhausted, too injured. He called Florida's Fish and Wildlife Conservation Commission. The workers there would know how to take care of a wounded dolphin.

Jim watched over the dolphin until the rescue team arrived a few hours later. As soon as they saw the cuts around the dolphin's tail, they knew they would need to move her somewhere safe so she could heal.

Even though she was injured, the dolphin was not easy to catch. But they finally corralled her. After lifting her from the lagoon, the rescue team tried to help her relax before carrying her to the transport van. They had a long drive ahead of them, all the way across Florida to the Clearwater Marine Aquarium.

Everyone worries that Winter is too weak to make the trip.

A small, anxious crowd awaited the dolphin's arrival at the aquarium. The group included a veterinarian, dolphin trainers, and volunteers. When the van pulled up, they were all ready to help. It had not been an easy journey. The dolphin had been out of the water for more than three hours. On top of that, the night air was cold. It was so chilly that the group decided to name the dolphin Winter.

The rescue workers carefully moved Winter to a holding tank. Abby, the head dolphin trainer, stood alongside Winter in the tank. Immediately, the veterinarian evaluated Winter's health. It was clear the little dolphin was badly injured. The vet estimated that Winter was only two or three months old. In the wild, baby dolphins drink their mother's milk until they are about two years old. Winter was so young that she would not know how to eat a fish if they offered it to her. But she needed food. The only choice was to gently insert a special feeding tube down her throat.

Winter was probably still scared from her ordeal so, although the tube did not hurt, she continued to struggle.

Abby and the rest of the aquarium staff knew, however, that it was good that Winter was struggling—it showed she still had the heart and energy to try to protect herself.

Volunteers remain with Winter around the clock to make sure her blowhole stays above the water.

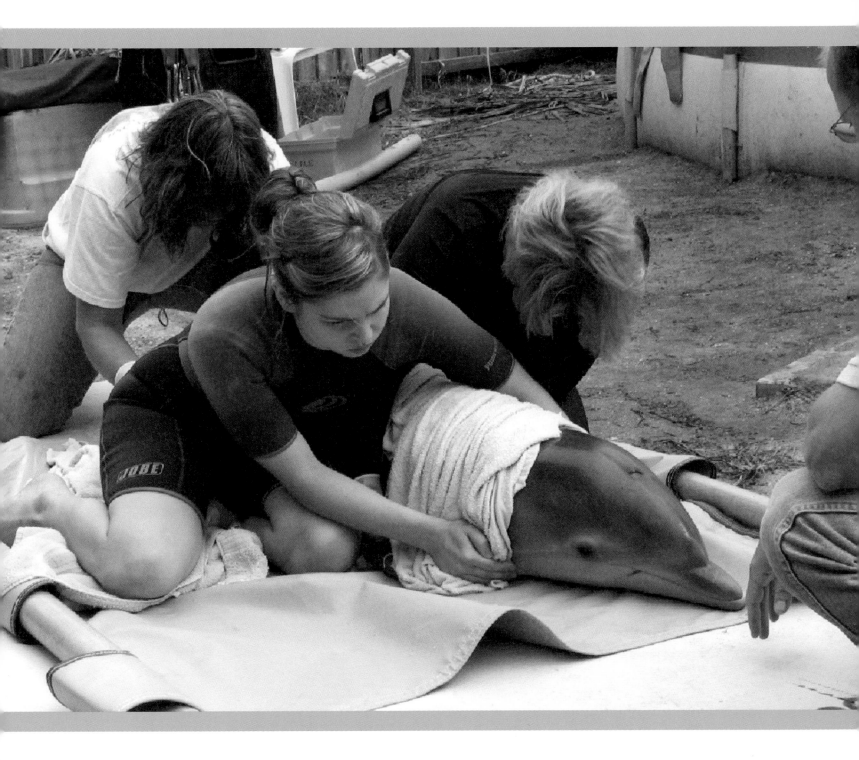

The tail's strength is what gives dolphins their tremendous speed. Without her tail, would Winter swim on her own again?

On Winter's second day at the aquarium, Abby showed her a bottle. The bottle contained a milk formula developed for zoo animals. At first, Winter did not know what the bottle was for. It took her a week to get the hang of drinking from it, and then the staff no longer needed to feed her with the tube. Each day, they weighed Winter. She started to gain weight. It was a good sign.

Winter was still very sick. The rope from the trap had been wrapped so tightly around her tail that it had stopped the blood flow. Pieces of her tail were starting to flake off, little by little.

Nonetheless, by the end of the week, Abby and the other trainers no longer felt they had to support Winter in the water. They encouraged her to swim on her own. And then, just as everyone feared, Winter lost her tail. What was left was a fleshy stump that would heal over time.

Would Winter be able to swim without her tail?

A volunteer coaxes Winter to drink from a bottle.

Winter did start to swim on her own, but she did not swim like other dolphins. Her tail stump swished from side to side, more like the motion of a fish or a shark than the up-and-down tail action of a dolphin. Still, it was amazing! Winter had taught herself an entirely new way to swim! Her trainers were impressed, but they were also concerned that she might damage her backbone by swimming the wrong way.

Although Winter's tail had fallen off, the wound had healed. She was getting used to her new home and her handlers. Whenever someone arrived next to her pool with a bottle, she gave a cheery welcome of clicks and whistles. By the time Winter was about five months old, she began daily training sessions with her handlers. They used training techniques similar to those used with the aquarium's other dolphins, and she learned to listen to their signals. Winter was a quick and enthusiastic learner.

Winter is still healing but, to the amazement of everyone, she can swim.

Winter had learned to trust the people who cared for her, but she had not seen another dolphin since arriving at the aquarium. Now it was time to meet a new friend. The trainers decided to introduce Winter to Panama, a female dolphin who had been rescued as well. The trainers were not sure how Winter would react to Panama—or how Panama would react to Winter. Would Panama even recognize Winter as a dolphin?

When they first brought Winter to the new tank, Panama kept her distance. Winter stayed by the edge, where she felt safest, and watched the older dolphin swim laps around the pool. But Winter got tired of waiting. If she wanted to make a friend, it was clear she would have to make it happen. Now, whenever Panama passed, Winter swam out to greet her. Panama tried to ignore Winter, but Winter was unfazed. She kept playfully approaching Panama. Finally, after three long days, Panama gave up. She stopped trying to swim away from Winter, and the two dolphins have been together ever since.

Winter and Panama are constant companions.

When Winter was about a year old, NBC's *The Today Show* broadcast a story about her on television. Now the word was out. Winter was famous. People started to come in droves to visit her at the Clearwater Marine Aquarium. The charming young dolphin also started to receive letters from her new fans, including many people who knew someone who had, or had themselves, lost or been born without a limb or had other disabilities. Everyone could relate to Winter.

Winter seemed to be able to overcome any obstacle. While her vets and trainers were happy that Winter was adjusting to her new life, they knew she was about to face her biggest challenge. Months of swimming from side to side had taken their toll. Abby helped Winter do special poolside exercises, but Winter's muscles were not as flexible and developed as they should have been. Winter needed to be able to swim like a dolphin again.

Luckily, Kevin Carroll heard about Winter on the radio and contacted the aquarium. Kevin was not only a dolphin lover, he was also a premier creator of prostheses—special devices that can help replace a body part such as an arm or a leg. Kevin believed he could help.

Every day, crowds come to see Winter the famous dolphin.

Kevin Carroll (left) and his team from Hanger Prosthetics & Orthotics face many challenges in devising the perfect tail for Winter.

Being a dolphin, Winter was a special case. Not only would her prosthesis have to work in the water, it would also have to handle the force of each thrust of her tail. A team of experts—including Kevin Carroll, vets, dolphin trainers, and marine mammal researchers—came together to help make Winter's new tail a reality.

Everyone shared ideas about how to create the best prosthesis for Winter. It was something that had never been done before, and there were many obstacles. The first was the fit. Winter did not have a tail joint or any other place for a prosthesis to attach to her body. In addition, dolphins have especially sensitive skin. The team would need to figure out how to connect the tail without causing irritation or discomfort to Winter. The second concern was the tail's function. They needed a design that would mimic the up-and-down movement of a swimming dolphin.

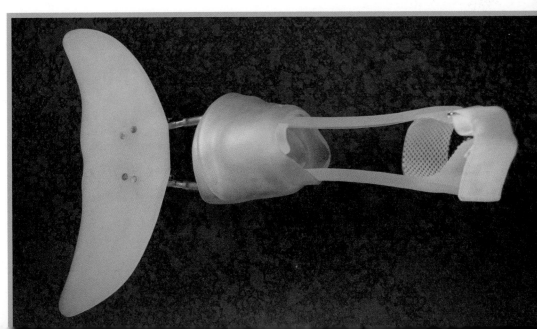

Winter's special tail

Finally, there was a concern for Winter herself. How would she react to wearing the tail? Abby and the other trainers worked tirelessly, preparing Winter. First they needed to help Winter get used to the feel of wearing a prosthesis. Then they could teach her how to swim with her own prosthetic tail.

The development team quickly realized they would have to create a sleeve designed specifically to fit Winter. They made a mold of her peduncle so the new sleeve would be a perfect fit. Then Kevin Carroll went one step further. He created

a special silicone gel that would be smooth against Winter's skin and would add a cushion to make the prosthesis more comfortable for Winter to wear.

It took several months and several designs for the team to develop a prosthetic sleeve and a tail that matched the natural motion of an actual dolphin tail. They ended up with a unique design. There would be two sleeves. The main silicone sleeve would fit right on Winter's peduncle. A second sleeve would fit on top of the first and would hold the tail and its brace in place.

Winter's tail needs to fit her just right so she can swim properly.

Winter shows off for the camera.

Abby spent many hours training Winter how to move her body while wearing the prosthetic tail. Abby needed Winter to understand that, when she was wearing the prosthesis, it was a signal for her to swim by using her tail, not her fins, to move herself forward.

Winter seems to like her new tail. She will sometimes swim in circles, chasing it, or show off by swimming right past Panama and flicking her tail in her friend's face. Some days, she doesn't want her trainers to take it off!

Winter now wears her tail every day for a short period of time. A trainer is always close by to keep an eye on her. The goal is for Winter to eventually wear the prosthesis a few hours every day, which will be enough to keep her backbone healthy and her body flexible. Even after Winter's first brief outings with the new tail, her trainers could already see an improvement.

Abby and fans eagerly watch Winter.

Birthday cards for Winter pour in from fans.

Winter had a big party on her third birthday, complete with a cake and candles. Many people came to help her celebrate, and she seemed happy to see them all.

We cannot know what Winter is really thinking, but her trainers admit that she seems to have a special understanding with the people who visit her. The people feel a connection to her as well. From children who have prostheses, to veterans who lost a limb fighting in a war, to one little girl who didn't want to wear a hearing aid until she met Winter, people see how Winter has learned to adapt and are inspired by her story.

With the help of Kevin Carroll, Winter is also sharing her prosthetic technology. After creating the silicone gel for her sleeve, Kevin realized that the same material that made it more comfortable for Winter to wear her prosthetic tail could help people who wear prostheses, too. Kevin put the gel to the test on a veteran of the Iraq war who was having difficulty with his artificial legs. The silicone gel created an extra cushion that helped reduce the veteran's discomfort. It was a big breakthrough, making life a little easier for people needing prostheses.

Special guests present Winter with her birthday cake!

Winter may have lost her family, her home, and eventually her tail, but she found a new home and family at the Clearwater Marine Aquarium. She found Panama, Abby, and the vets, trainers, and volunteers who take care of her on a daily basis. With the help of all of these people, she also has a new tail. Through these changes, one thing has stayed the same: Winter's uplifting spirit and her resilience have helped her adjust and make the most of every situation.

And her story is far from over. She is still learning all of the things she can do with her special tail, and her trainers and prosthetic designers are still learning how they can help her even more. Every step of the way, they will need to be open to new ideas and be willing to try different solutions. Their shared goal is to help Winter live a long, healthy, and happy life.

As for Winter, she seems ready for any new challenge. As champion, inspiration, and friend, Winter is one little dolphin who gives people hope and shows us that anything is possible.

Winter's Journey

Winter was rescued in Mosquito Lagoon and then transported in a special van all the way across Florida to the Clearwater Marine Aquarium. The trip was 165 miles long and kept Winter out of water for more than three hours. It was not an easy journey for the little dolphin but, with help from others and Winter's can-do attitude, she now is thriving at her new home.

Clearwater Marine Aquarium

www.SeeWinter.com

Founded in 1972, the Clearwater Marine Aquarium (CMA) is the world's most recognized marine life rescue center, dedicated to the rescue, rehabilitation, and release of injured, sick, or stranded marine life. This nonprofit organization, located in Clearwater, Florida, educates residents, visiting tourists, and millions more around the world via its global media presence on the importance of protecting and preserving our waters and marine life. CMA also oversees the area's sea turtle nesting program, combing miles of beaches during nesting season to ensure nests are located and cared for, and that hatchlings safely make it to the water. CMA staff and volunteers are on call 24/7 to rescue stranded or injured sea turtles, dolphins, river otters, and more.

Once an animal arrives at CMA's hospital, a team of experienced staff biologists, veterinarians, and volunteers create a rehabilitation plan for the animal, catering to its specific injuries or illnesses. Sometimes, as with Winter, the injuries are so severe that the animal would not survive on its own in the wild and therefore cannot ever be released. CMA works with agencies such as the National Marine Fisheries and the Florida Fish and Wildlife Conservation Commission to make these decisions. If an animal is unable to be released back into its natural environment, it becomes a lifelong resident of the Clearwater Marine Aquarium.

In spite of tremendous growth and a global presence, CMA remains a "neighborhood" aquarium, a place where children and adults alike can visit anytime to wonder at the unending diversity, grace, and beauty of the creatures of the sea. Environmental education plays an important role in the aquarium's marine life outreach. In addition to sharing their expertise and amazing animal rehabilitation stories, staff and volunteers work diligently to teach people how they can help protect marine animals from injuries. CMA conveys this important message through a variety of hands-on educational opportunities, including eco-boat tours, kids' camps, tours, off-site presentations, and animal interactions. CMA's wide-screen theater provides guests with films and behind-the-scenes footage of animal rescue, rehabilitation, and release.

Chief Executive Officer David Yates began working at CMA in February 2006. In a short period of time, his leadership propelled the aquarium to places it had never been. As the former CEO of the Ironman Triathlon, he has extensive experience in innovative thinking and leading people. Mr. Yates facilitated and managed the intensive process of helping Winter get a prosthetic tail. Since his arrival, attendance has skyrocketed, CMA's volunteer base has increased dramatically, and the CMA has experienced unparalleled global attention.

Dolphins

There are nearly forty different kinds of dolphins, living in all oceans and some rivers. They are closely related to whales and porpoises. Winter is an Atlantic bottlenose dolphin, which is one of the most common species. Dolphins are marine mammals. They breathe air like people do, but are uncomfortable being out of the water for an extended period of time. Dolphins breathe through the blowhole at the top of their head, and they come to surface often in graceful leaps from the water. This practice is called porpoising.

Bottlenose dolphins are extremely social, living in groups of up to fifteen dolphins. Several groups may join together for minutes or for hours, especially as they swim into deeper waters.

All dolphins use echolocation, which is a way of gaining information about the surrounding world by using sound. Dolphins emit a series of clicking noises, and then listen to how the clicks bounce back. The dolphin's brain processes the clicks, which give the dolphin important information: Echolocation can tell a dolphin about an object's size, shape, distance, speed, and direction. This skill is especially important when hunting in dark waters. Clicking, along with whistles and body posture, is also a way dolphins communicate with one another.

There are many accounts of dolphins helping to direct lost ships, and even beached pygmy sperm whales, to safer waters. Dolphins have also been known to protect swimmers from sharks.

Since dolphins live in the water, they are affected by the health of the world's oceans and rivers. When the waters are polluted, the pollution affects all marine life.

Training Dolphins

Atlantic bottlenose dolphins are well known for their intelligence, making them popular performers at marine parks, aquariums, and zoos. Dolphin trainers study marine biology for years to be able to train and care for dolphins in captivity. Like any relationship, the one between a trainer and a dolphin is based on trust and understanding. The trainer must gain that trust over time.

While it is fun to watch the dolphins perform, many of their "stunts" are intended to help handlers detect if a dolphin is injured or sick. A training session is a well-planned routine that allows the handler to see if the dolphin is behaving in her or his typical way. Trainers also work with dolphins to provide both physical and mental challenges. In the wild, dolphins swim fast to escape sharks or chase fish for dinner. It is good exercise, but in an aquarium, there is no threat of sharks and the dolphins do not have to catch their own food. Also, there is not the variety of outside stimulation found in the ocean and rivers. Trainers teach dolphins to swim fast and follow instructions in order to keep them healthy in body and mind.

Handlers use positive reinforcement in training dolphins. When the dolphin responds properly, the handler commends the dolphin and often offers a reward. The most primary and immediate reward is food, but other examples are toys, a nice rub, or a swim with the trainer. Trainers also use whistles. At the moment a dolphin does something correctly, the trainer blows a whistle and then follows it with a reward. Over time, the dolphin learns that the sound of a whistle is a sign that he or she is responding correctly. In this practice, the whistle is called a bridge because it connects the dolphin's actions to the eventual reward.

The handlers do not react to a dolphin's negative actions, which means they do not punish or reprimand the dolphins in any way. Marine specialists have learned that positive reinforcement is the most effective technique.

Handlers try to challenge the dolphins while maintaining a feeling of fun as well. With Winter, her trainers wanted to make sure they did not ask too much of her. They did not want her to perform a maneuver that was uncomfortable for her, so they first watched how she "played" in her free time. They noticed that Winter enjoyed porpoising, doing barrel rolls and somersaults, and swimming upright in the water. During training sessions, they asked her to repeat these behaviors, rewarding her when she learned to do them on cue.

Kevin Carroll and Hanger Prosthetics & Orthotics

Hanger Prosthetics & Orthotics was founded in 1861 by James Edward Hanger, the first amputee of the American Civil War. After being unable to find a suitable prosthetic leg, Mr. Hanger set out to create one for himself. His wooden artificial limb design—with a hinge at the knee—was so successful that the government paid him to build prosthetic limbs for other veterans.

Today, nearly 150 years later, Hanger Prosthetics & Orthotics is still revolutionizing the industry. Kevin Carroll, a vice president of the company, has engineered replacement limbs for veterans, athletes, and animals, giving all his patients the individual care necessary to help them achieve their goals.

Kevin Carroll is energized by his job, and he likes the challenge of helping amputees overcome their limitations. He is known for combining his compassion, humor, and skill in working with individuals. Being an animal lover, he approached the Clearwater Marine Aquarium, believing he could help Winter. Even though it was a far more extensive endeavor than he had imagined, Carroll and his team of experts, including a Hanger practitioner named Dan Strzempka, who is also an amputee, like Winter, worked through many sleeves and designs to best fit Winter and her growing body.

After developing the silicone gel that reduced irritation on Winter's sensitive skin, Carroll realized that it would also reduce the friction on human skin. Similarly, when engineers create prostheses for competitive athletes, the technology benefits everyone. After attending the Beijing Paralympics, Carroll emphasized the need for amputees to get out in the world and be active. He noted that both the Challenged Athletes Foundation and Disabled Sports USA offer individuals opportunities to become athletic again—and not just at a competitive level. These are supportive communities, and Kevin Carroll feels it is part of his job as a clinician to help make people aware of their possibilities.